Oceans
INSIDE OUT

Robin Johnson

CRABTREE
Publishing Company
www.crabtreebooks.com

Author: Robin Johnson
Publishing plan research
  and series development: Reagan Miller
Editorial director: Kathy Middleton
Editors: Sarah Eason, Jennifer Sanderson,
  Nancy Dickmann, and Shirley Duke
Proofreader: Wendy Scavuzzo
Project coordinator: Sarah Eason
Design: Paul Myerscough
Photo research: Rachel Blount
Production coordinator and
  Prepress technician: Tammy McGarr
Print coordinator: Katherine Berti

Written, developed, and produced by Calcium

Photo Credits:

t=Top, bl=Bottom Left, br=Bottom Right

Dreamstime: Michal Bednare: p. 6–7; Richard Carey: p. 4–5; Chriswood4: p. 14–15; Divehive: p. 10–11, p. 22–23; Stefan Pircher: p. 26–27; James Wheeler: p. 3, p. 18–19. FLPA: Norbert Wu/Minden Pictures: p. 13 (br). Nature Picture Library: Doug Perrine: p. 20–21. NOAA: Hidden Ocean 2005 Expedition: NOAA Office of Ocean Exploration: p. 15 (tr); NOAA MESA Project: p. 11 (tr). Shutterstock: Aquapix: p. 23 (tr); Rich Carey: p. 12–13; Mark Caunt: p. 9 (br); David Evison: p. 24–25; Andrea Izzotti: p. 8–9; Brian Kinney: p. 28–29; Littlesam: p. 1, p. 16–17; Nagel Photography: p. 21 (br); Galushko Sergey: p. 19 (tr); Specta: p. 1 (br); Vlada Z: p. 17 (br); Paul S. Wolf: p. 25 (br); Worldswildlifewonders: p. 27 (br).

Cover: Shutterstock: RWBrooks; Bluehand (br).

Library and Archives Canada Cataloguing in Publication

Johnson, Robin (Robin R.), author
    Oceans inside out / Robin Johnson.

(Ecosystems inside out)
Includes index.
Issued in print and electronic formats.
ISBN 978-0-7787-0635-9 (bound).--
ISBN 978-0-7787-1457-6 (pbk.).--
ISBN 978-1-4271-7648-6 (pdf).--ISBN 978-1-4271-7642-4 (html)

    1. Marine ecology--Juvenile literature. 2. Marine animals--Juvenile literature. I. Title.

QH541.5.S3J64 2014   j577.7   C2014-903621-3
                                           C2014-903622-1

Library of Congress Cataloging-in-Publication Data

Johnson, Robin (Robin R.), author.
  Oceans inside out / Robin Johnson.
       pages cm. -- (Ecosystems inside out)
  Includes index.
  ISBN 978-0-7787-0635-9 (reinforced library binding) --
ISBN 978-0-7787-1457-6 (pbk.) --
ISBN 978-1-4271-7648-6 (electronic pdf) --
ISBN 978-1-4271-7642-4 (electronic html)
1. Marine ecology--Juvenile literature. 2. Ocean--Juvenile literature. 3. Oceanography--Juvenile literature. I. Title.

QH541.5.S3J65 2015
577.7--dc23
                                           2014020250

Crabtree Publishing Company

www.crabtreebooks.com   1-800-387-7650

Printed in Hong Kong/082014/BK20140613

Published in Canada
Crabtree Publishing
616 Welland Ave.
St. Catharines, Ontario
L2M 5V6

Published in the United States
Crabtree Publishing
PMB 59051
350 Fifth Avenue, 59th Floor
New York, New York 10118

Published in the United Kingdom
Crabtree Publishing
Maritime House
Basin Road North, Hove
BN41 1WR

Published in Australia
Crabtree Publishing
3 Charles Street
Coburg North
VIC, 3058

Contents

What Is an Ecosystem?

An **ecosystem** is made up of **organisms**, the environment in which they live, and their **interrelationships**. Each plant and animal depends on other living and nonliving things in the ecosystem for its survival. Living things are called **biotic factors**. Nonliving things such as water, sunlight, and air, are called **abiotic factors**. The plants and animals that survive in an ecosystem depend on the biotic and abiotic factors that exist there.

Sizes of Ecosystems

Ecosystems can be large or small. Some are as small as puddles, while others are as huge as the deep, blue sea. A **biome** is a large geographical area that contains similar plants, animals, and environments. Oceans, rain forests, and tundras are examples of biomes.

What Is an Ocean?

An ocean is a large area of salt water. **Oceanographers** divide the water on Earth into five oceans—Pacific, Atlantic, Indian, Southern, and Arctic. However, there is really only one huge area of water on Earth. Strong **currents** carry water from ocean to ocean. They also take some of the plants and animals along for the ride.

Let's jump in and look at each **marine** ecosystem as a whole, then dive deeper into one part of it!

What Is a System?

A **system** is a group of separate parts that work together for a purpose. The abiotic conditions in each part of the ecosystem determine the kind of life that can survive there. Plants, animals, water, temperature, and soil are some of the parts of ecosystems. Each biotic and abiotic factor has a specific and important role that helps the ecosystem function.

A healthy ecosystem has many types of plants and animals whose needs are met by the parts of the ecosystem. Ecosystems exist in a delicate balance. A change to just one part of an ecosystem affects all the other parts of the ecosystem.

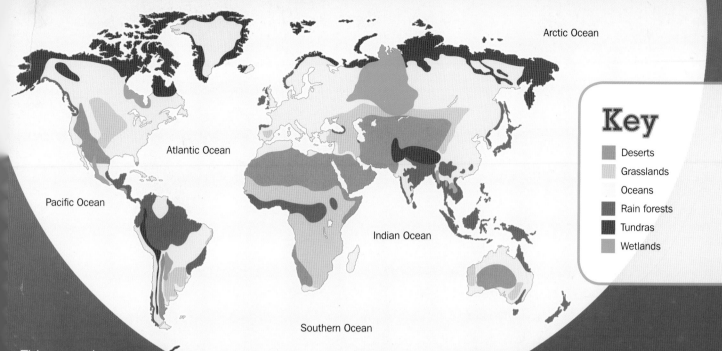

Key

- Deserts
- Grasslands
- Oceans
- Rain forests
- Tundras
- Wetlands

Arctic Ocean

Atlantic Ocean

Pacific Ocean

Indian Ocean

Southern Ocean

This map shows where oceans and other biomes are found around the world.

Sharks and other fish in the sea depend on a system of biotic and abiotic factors for their survival.

Energy in Ecosystems

sun

From tiny plants to enormous blue whales, every living thing in an ocean ecosystem needs **energy** to survive. Energy comes from food. A **food chain** shows how an organism gets food, and how this energy is then passed from one organism to another. Many different organisms rely on a single food chain.

The Flow of Energy

Living things in an ecosystem can be producers, consumers, or decomposers. Plants have **chlorophyll** and are called producers because they use energy from the sun to produce their own food through a process called **photosynthesis**.

Animals are consumers. They must eat food to get energy to survive. Primary consumers are animals that eat plants. They are also called herbivores. Manatees and dugongs are large marine herbivores. Secondary consumers, such as sharks and killer whales, are carnivores that eat animals for food. Omnivores eat both plants and animals.

Decomposers are organisms that break down dead plants and animal matter. Like nature's recyclers, they put **nutrients** back into the oceans so that food chains can begin again.

Food Webs

Energy does not stay in just one food chain. It flows to living things in many other food chains. When two or more food chains connect, they create a **food web**. A healthy food web provides energy for many **species**, or types, of plants and animals in an ecosystem.

sea grass

dugong

tiger shark

This food chain shows the flow of energy from one organism to another.

Like all marine animals, these fish must consume food to get the energy they need to survive.

Eco Up Close

All living things need water to survive. Water changes form and moves around the world through a process called the water cycle, much of it powered by the ocean's **evaporation**. The other parts of the cycle are **condensation** and **precipitation**. As water moves around Earth, it brings along anything that is in it. If **pollutants** enter the water, they can easily be carried from one marine ecosystem to another. This damages and can even destroy ecosystems.

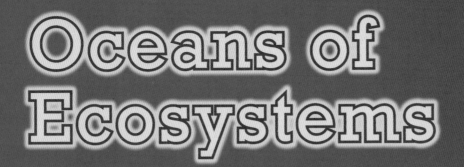

Oceans of Ecosystems

There are many different ecosystems in the oceans around the world. Some oceans have icy waters all year long, while others are warmed by **tropical** sunshine. Some oceans have plenty of fish for **predators** to eat, while others have very little **prey**. Predators hunt and kill other animals for food. Prey are the animals they catch and eat. All animals in an ecosystem are interdependent, which means they rely on one another and plants for their survival.

Many Different Systems

There are also different ecosystems in different parts of oceans. In some ecosystems, marine animals climb out of the water onto rocky shores each day or live attached to rocky shores or in small pools of salt water formed by waves splashing. In other ecosystems, animals never leave the murky, deep ocean.

Suited for Salt Water

Marine plants and animals have **adapted** to the abiotic and biotic factors of each ocean ecosystem. To adapt is to change over a very long period of time to better suit an environment. All marine plants and animals have adapted to live in salt water. However, different organisms must also adapt to different water temperatures, depths, and **pressure**, as well as different amounts of sunlight, air, and salinity, or saltiness. Water is always moving, so ocean **habitats** are always changing in some ways. A habitat is the natural environment where a plant or animal lives.

Dugongs and other marine animals have adapted to live in the warm, shallow waters of some oceans.

Eco Up Close

Most fish have adapted to live in either salt water or **fresh water**. Fresh water does not contain a lot of salt. It is found in lakes, ponds, rivers, and streams around the world. Salmon have adapted to live in both saltwater and freshwater habitats, however. Salmon hatch from eggs in freshwater streams. They **migrate**, or travel, to the ocean to find food. After a few years in the salty open ocean, salmon return to freshwater streams to lay eggs and **reproduce** and finish their **life cycles**.

salmon

In the Zone

Sunlight, an abiotic factor, powers the ocean biome. It shines down on oceans and warms the surface of the water. The sun's rays cannot reach all the way to the bottom of oceans, however. Many parts of the oceans are about 14,000 feet (4,267 m) deep, but there are places that are more than twice that deep! Oceanographers divide the **water column** into layers, or light zones. Each zone receives a different amount of light and energy from the sun. The deeper you go, the less light there is. Different organisms have adapted to survive in each zone.

Sunny Side Up

The top layer of the ocean is called the sunlit, or photic, zone. Photic means "light" in Greek. The sun bathes the top 656 feet (200 m) of the ocean in sunlight. These warm waters are home to most ocean organisms. The sun shines brightly there, so photosynthesis can take place.

With plenty of plants to eat, the sunlit zone is a suitable habitat for many different types of marine animals. Sharks, dolphins, whales, tuna, sea turtles, and countless other ocean animals make their homes there.

Many animals that live in the sunlit zone have countershading. Their bodies are light on the bottom and dark on top. Countershading helps the animals blend in with the sunny waters above them and the dark waters below.

phytoplankton

Eco Up Close

Phytoplankton are found at the bottom of all marine food chains. They are **microscopic algae** that grow in the sunlit zone of oceans. Algae are plant-like organisms that have chlorophyll and use sunlight to make food. Algae are not true plants because, unlike plants, they do not have roots that hold them in place and absorb nutrients. Billions of phytoplankton float on the oceans' surface. They are primary producers that feed consumers. Fish and other small animals eat phytoplankton. Larger fish and marine **mammals** eat the small animals. Without phytoplankton, there would be no living things in oceans.

Where the Sun Doesn't Shine

Below the sunlit zone is the deep sea. It is a huge, dark, cold area of water. Oceanographers divide the deep sea into two zones. The twilight zone stretches from the bottom of the sunlit zone to 3,300 feet (1,006 m) below the surface. The twilight zone is also called the disphotic (meaning "poorly lit") zone. It receives a little light, but not enough for photosynthesis to take place. The midnight, or aphotic (meaning "no light") zone continues to the bottom of the ocean. There, it is pitch black, the water temperature is just above freezing, and the water pressure is high. No plants and very few animals can survive in these waters.

Deep-Sea Divers

Animals that live in the deep sea have adapted to the harsh abiotic conditions. Some, such as sea jellies, octopuses, and squids, have soft bodies that can withstand high water pressure. Others, such as eels and bristlemouths, have thin, dark bodies that **camouflage** them in dark waters.

Finding Food

Many deep-sea predators have large eyes and a strong sense of smell to help them find prey in low light. Some animals migrate up the water column to find food, but most depend on **marine snow** for energy. Marine snow is a shower of nutrient-rich **detritus** that falls from the sunlit zone high above. **Bacteria** and other ocean decomposers break down the detritus and release important nutrients back into the water.

This cuttlefish has large eyes for finding food in the dark waters of the deep sea.

Eco Up Close

Anglerfish are deep-sea carnivores that have a bright way to catch prey. They have body parts that rise above their mouths and glow in dark ocean waters. The glow attracts predators, which soon become prey for the anglerfish. Anglerfish have huge mouths and stomachs. They can gobble up animals twice their size. Consuming large prey gives anglerfish enough energy to survive long periods of time between meals.

anglerfish

Icy Waters

The water at the bottom of all oceans is icy cold. However, in the Arctic Ocean and Southern Ocean, the water on top is even colder! In fact, a layer of **sea ice** covers parts of these oceans all year long. The water freezes because polar oceans are found in the coldest places on Earth. The Arctic Ocean is found in the north polar region, and the Southern Ocean surrounds Antarctica. Both places have very cold **climates**. Animals that live in these icy oceans have adapted to the freezing temperatures. Many have layers of fat called blubber to keep them warm. Some have warm feathers or fur.

Polar bears are skilled hunters that help control the populations of many species in the Arctic Ocean ecosystem. Their white fur helps camouflage the big bears in the snow and ice while they hunt.

On Thin Ice

Polar oceans are home to many **hardy** animals, including polar bears. Polar bears live on sea ice in the Arctic Ocean. From the ice, they hunt seals, walruses, narwhals, and beluga whales. Polar bears are apex predators. They are at the top of the food chain and have few or no natural predators.

Although they do not face predators, polar bears do face another threat. **Climate change** is melting sea ice in polar oceans. If their habitat shrinks or disappears, polar bears are in danger of dying out. Without apex predators, the **populations** of other species will grow out of control and disrupt the ecosystem.

krill

Eco Up Close

Antarctic krill are small shrimp-like creatures that are around just 2.4 inches (6 cm) long. They live in the Southern Ocean. They are a keystone species. A keystone species is one that plays such an important role in its environment that it affects many other organisms. Antarctic krill feed on phytoplankton and ice algae. In turn, krill are an important food source for many whales, penguins, seals, squid, fish, and other animals in the Southern Ocean.

Eco Focus

Antarctic krill feed on ice algae that grow in sea ice. Shrinking sea ice will result in fewer krill. How could smaller numbers of a keystone species such as krill affect the entire ocean biome?

15

Temperate Oceans

Temperate oceans are found between the polar regions and the **tropics**. They include parts of the Atlantic Ocean, Indian Ocean, and Pacific Ocean. Temperate oceans have temperate, or mild, temperatures that change with the seasons. The climate is hot in the summer and cold in the winter. The abiotic conditions in the oceans suit the needs of many plant and animal species.

Mix It Up

In the summer, the sun heats the surface of temperate oceans and allows many plants to grow. This warm, bright layer of water is separated from the cold, dark water below by the **thermocline**. The thermocline is an invisible boundary, or dividing line, between waters that have very different temperatures.

In the winter, the temperature drops and the surface water cools. The thermocline disappears and the surface water mixes with the cold waters below. Deep water contains nutrients that have fallen from the sunlit zone and that algae need to make food. The mixing of warm surface water with cooler water below brings nutrients back to the surface, where photosynthesis takes place.

Plenty of Fish in the Sea

With so many plants and animals to eat, temperate oceans have huge fish populations. They are home to cod, tuna, halibut, haddock, herring, mackerel, salmon, and many other types of fish. Many fish species swim together in large groups called schools. Swimming in schools helps fish find food and **mates**, and avoid predators. It does not prevent them from being caught, however. **Commercial trawlers** spot schools of fish and cast huge nets to catch them.

Eco Focus

Laws and regulations were put into place so that certain species of fish can be caught only at certain times of the year to keep their populations healthy. Yet the world's population is growing and the need for food, especially fish, is putting more strain on ocean fishing grounds. What arguments could be made for or against regulating the fishing, especially with trawlers using huge nets? Is there another answer to this problem?

Many fish have adapted to living in temperate oceans by swimming in huge schools. This helps them because predators cannot single out one fish.

Eco Up Close

Atlantic cod are large, brown-green, spotted fish that were once **abundant** in the Atlantic Ocean. **Overfishing** greatly reduced their populations. Overfishing is taking too many of one species from a certain area. Atlantic cod are now **endangered**.

Atlantic cod

On the Rocks

Water from oceans crashes onto rocky shores. It moves forward and backward throughout the day with the changing **tides**. Organisms that live in rocky-shore ecosystems must adapt to pounding waves, changing temperatures, and varying amounts of water, air, sunlight, and salt. They must protect themselves from predators in the water and on the land. It is a harsh environment in which only the toughest plants and animals can survive.

One Zone, Four Parts

The place where the ocean meets the shore is called the **intertidal zone**. Oceanographers divide the intertidal zone into four parts—the spray zone at the top of the rocks, the high tide zone, the middle tide zone, and the low tide zone at the bottom. As water moves in and out with the tides, different areas are covered with water.

A Tough Life

Different plants and animals have adapted to live in each part of the intertidal zone. The spray zone is mostly dry, and very few plants grow there. The low tide zone is mostly wet, so surf grass, sea lettuce, and other marine plants and algae can grow there. Limpets, barnacles, and mussels are tough creatures that cling or attach tightly to rocks throughout the intertidal zone. They have hard shells that help protect them from predators. Others have strong limbs that grip the rocks and keep them from being washed away.

Eco Up Close

Sea stars are the stars of rocky seashores. These marine animals have hard body armor to protect them from crabs, seagulls, sea otters, and other predators. If a sea star loses an arm to a predator, a new arm grows in its place! Sea stars are **opportunistic feeders**, which means they will eat just about anything they find. They are a keystone species because their varied diet helps control the populations of many different seashore animals.

sea star

Tide pools form on rocky shores when the tides move out. They are harsh habitats for sea urchins, sea anemones, sea stars, and many other sea creatures. As the tides move in and out these hardy organisms face different water levels and temperatures, and other changing abiotic factors.

Tropical Oceans

Tropical oceans are clear, warm waters found near the equator in the tropics. They include the central parts of the Pacific Ocean and Atlantic Ocean, and most of the Indian Ocean. The climate in the tropics is hot all year, with plenty of sunshine.

Little to Eat

You might think that warm temperatures and plenty of sunlight would mean great **biodiversity** in tropical oceans. However, there are few living things in the open waters of these oceans. The surface of tropical oceans stays warm and bright all year, so there is a constant thermocline between the surface waters and the cold waters below. The waters never mix, so nutrients remain trapped below the thermocline. Without nutrients, plants cannot produce food. Without producers, there is no food for consumers to eat.

Go with the Flow

Animals that live in tropical oceans have adapted to the small amounts of food in their habitats. Some animals migrate to temperate waters where there is plenty of food. They travel long distances to feed, then return to tropical waters. Some animals follow strong currents to reach cold waters, while others stay in tropical oceans and feed in the currents that pass through the oceans. Others, such as the giant clam, rely on a **mutualistic relationship** with brightly colored algae to provide food. The currents carry warm water from the equator to the polar regions and bring cold, nutrient-rich water back to the equator.

Spiny lobsters form long chains as they migrate across the ocean floor. This adaptation keeps them safer because predators are less likely to attack them in groups.

The warm Alaskan current is found on Canada's west coast, while on the east coast, the warm Gulf Stream stretches from Florida in the United States to Newfoundland.

Key

→ warm water current

← cold water current

Eco Up Close

Humboldt penguins are birds that feed in tropical waters off the coast of Peru. They feed on anchovies, sardines, and other small fish that are carried north in a cold, slow-moving current called the Humboldt Current. Humboldt penguins travel great distances to find food when there is little food in their habitat.

Humboldt penguin

Coral Reefs

Coral reefs are huge underwater structures that mostly grow in warm, shallow waters on the coasts of tropical oceans. Tiny, soft-bodied animals called coral polyps make coral reefs. Coral polyps use **minerals** in the water to build hard, protective skeletons around their bodies. When the coral polyps die, their skeletons remain in the ocean. Over time, the skeletons pile up and form huge, rock-like coral reefs. Groups of living coral polyps, called corals, live at the top of coral reefs.

Working Together

Like all living things, corals need nutrients to grow. There are few nutrients in tropical oceans, so the plants and animals in coral reefs must work together to survive. Coral polyps and algae have a mutalistic relationship that forms the basis of coral reefs. Tiny algae live inside the bodies of coral polyps. This keeps the algae safe from hungry herbivores. The algae use nutrients in the waste of coral polyps to make food, which is eaten by the coral.

Sharing and Growing

The sharing of nutrients by algae and coral keeps coral reefs growing and provides a great habitat for many species. Seahorses, barracudas, sharks, hawksbill turtles, puffer fish, sponges, and many other animals find food and shelter among the corals. The animals release nutrients in their waste. Plants in coral reefs use the nutrients to produce more food for the animals to eat.

clownfish

Eco Up Close

Clownfish and sea anemones have a mutualistic relationship. Sea anemones have a poisonous sting that can kill many fish, but not clownfish. Clownfish have a coating that allows them to swim safely among the deadly sea anemones. Sea anemones protect clownfish from predators. In return, the Clownfish clean waste from the sea anemones. The colorful fish also attract animals that want to eat them, but the animals are instead caught and eaten by the sea anemones.

Coral reefs are busy, colorful habitats for hawksbill turtles, fish, and many other marine animals.

Sandy Shores

Coastal areas have sandy shores made up of tiny grains of sand or crushed shells. They are found on the edges of oceans around the world. Like rocky shores, sandy shores are dangerous places for plants and animals. Crashing waves, changing tides, high winds, and other abiotic factors make them harsh habitats.

Changing to Survive

Despite the challenges, many plants and animals have adapted to live in sandy-shore ecosystems. Some organisms, such as crabs, sandhoppers, and sea snails, live on sandy shores throughout the year. They dig in the sand to hide from predators and to keep from being washed away.

Just Visiting

Organisms, such as sea turtles and seabirds, live on sandy shores for just part of the year. They find food and build their nests there, but do not stay for long.

Sea turtles live mainly in shallow coastal waters. They **graze** on sea grass on the sea floor, which helps keep the plants healthy. Sea grass must be kept short so it can grow. Male sea turtles spend their lives in the ocean, but female sea turtles go to sandy shores to lay their eggs. They dig holes in the sand, lay eggs inside the holes, fill them with sand, then return to the sea. The sand hides the eggs from predators, while nutrients from the eggs nourish plants that grow on the beach.

Female sea turtles lay between 50 and 200 eggs in the sand. Baby sea turtles hatch from the eggs and make their way slowly to the ocean. Along the way, they are prey for hungry seagulls.

Eco Up Close

Seagulls are seabirds that live on seashores. They travel across beaches and coastal waters, searching for food. Seagulls hunt fish, crabs, rodents, and insects. Seagulls are also **scavengers**. Scavengers are animals that eat dead animals that they did not kill. Scavengers are important to ecosystems because they clean up waste and break it down into smaller pieces that decompose more quickly.

seagull

Ocean Forests

Kelp forests are thick **aquatic** forests made of giant, brown algae called kelp. The kelp make food by photosynthesis but, unlike plants, have no roots or true leaves. They anchor to the ocean floor with **holdfasts**. The kelp grow near the shores of cold oceans. Many are found on the west coast of North America.

Home in the Forest

Kelp forests are full of life! They provide food and shelter for thousands of marine species. Many animals hunt prey and hide from predators among the long, wavy blades of kelp. Sea otters, sea lions, seals, whales, kelp bass, rockfish, and giant kelpfish are some of the many animals that make their homes in kelp forests.

Mangrove Trees

Mangroves are hardy trees that grow along tropical oceans. Unlike most trees, mangroves have adapted to drink salt water and grow in soil that has little oxygen. Some mangrove species have roots that grow above the ground and take in oxygen from the air. Other species have roots that remove salt from the water.

Tropical coasts depend on mangroves. The thick, tangled roots of mangrove trees block ocean waves and help prevent coastal **erosion**. They also provide habitats for tropical plants and animals. Unfortunately, mangrove forests in southeast Asia and other parts of the world are being destroyed so that people can build fish and shrimp farms in their place.

Thousands of species find food and make their homes in underwater kelp forests.

26

Eco Focus

Each year, people destroy about 370,050 acres (149,754 ha) of mangrove forest, leaving coasts open to erosion. How could damage to coastal ecosystems affect the ocean biome?

sea otter

Eco Up Close

Sea otters are a keystone species in kelp forests. They are carnivores that eat sea urchins and other **invertebrates** on the sea floor. Sea urchins graze on the lower parts of the kelp, which causes the upper parts of the kelp to drift away and die. By feeding on sea urchins, sea otters control their populations and help the kelp—as well as the entire ecosystem it supports.

Sink or Swim

Oceans are vital to all living things. They move water around the world as a key part of the water cycle. They also help control Earth's climates. They absorb heat from the sun and spread that energy around the world. Oceans provide food for countless animals in complex food webs. They are home to more than 225,000 species and a variety of ecosystems. However, ocean ecosystems are in trouble—and their survival depends on everyone.

What Can You Do?

Clean up trash from seashores. Never leave your garbage behind when you visit coastal areas.

Never pick plants or disturb animals or nests that you find near oceans.

Avoid polluting. Try not to use chemicals and other pollutants that end up in oceans. Dispose of them properly at recycling centers.

Help the oceans by thinking of other ways you can help protect marine plants and animals. Then spread the word and keep ocean ecosystems flowing.

Activity:

Be a Clean-Up Crew!

Did you know that oil and water do not mix? This activity proves it! It also shows how hard it is to clean oceans when **oil spills** occur.

You Will Need:

- Clear bowl
- Water
- Food coloring
- Spoon
- 1 teaspoon (5 ml) of cooking oil
- Length of yarn or string

Instructions

1. Pour water into the bowl until it is half full.
2. Add a few drops of food coloring and stir the water until it changes color.
3. Pour the cooking oil into the bowl. The oil will float on the surface of the water.

oil

water

The Challenge

Now try to remove the oil from the water. Brainstorm to come up with different solutions. What materials could you use to absorb the oil? What tools could you use to skim the oil off the top? Could you add something to break down or **dilute** the oil? Test your ideas and record the results. Next, dip a length of yarn or string in the liquid and push it to the bottom with a spoon. Then pull it out and try to clean it. What did you notice? How would animals in oil be affected?

Consider the following questions

Would your solutions also work to clean up massive oil spills in the ocean? Why or why not?

Glossary

Please note: Some bold-faced words are defined in the text

abiotic factors Nonliving parts of an ecosystem, such as water and soil

abundant Plentiful; having a good supply or large population

aquatic Describing something that lives in, on, or near water

bacteria Living organisms made up of only one cell

biodiversity The variety of plant and animal life in an ecosystem or other area on Earth

biotic factors Living parts of an ecosystem, such as plants and animals

camouflage To blend in with the surroundings

chlorophyll A green substance in plants that changes sunlight and carbon dioxide into energy, which is stored as sugar and used by the plant for food

climate change A process in which the environment changes to become warmer, colder, drier, or wetter than normal. This can occur naturally, or it can be caused by human activity

climates The usual weather in specific areas

commercial trawlers Ships that catch and sell fish and other marine animals

condensation The process in which water vapor cools and changes to liquid form

currents Strong movements of water in a certain direction

detritus Dead plant and animal matter that is broken down by decomposers

dilute To make a liquid thinner or weaker by adding water or another liquid

ecosystem A group of living and nonliving things that live and interact in an area

endangered At risk of dying out

energy The power that nutrients from food provide to the body

erosion The process in which soil and rocks are worn away by water and wind over time

evaporation The process in which water is heated by the sun and changed from a liquid into a gas called water vapor

food chain A chain of organisms in which each member uses the member below as food

food web The interlinked food chains in an ecosystem

graze To feed on plants or algae

hardy Able to stand up to harsh conditions

holdfasts A stalk that keeps certain aquatic plants and animals anchored to the sea floor

interrelationships The relationships between many different organisms and their environment

invertebrates Animals that do not have backbones

life cycles Changes that take place from the time an organism begins its life until it is an adult that can reproduce

mammals Warm-blooded animals that have lungs, a backbone, and hair or fur, and drink milk from their mother's body

marine Found in the ocean

marine snow Waste found in the oceans that is rich in nutrients

mates Partners that animals need so they can reproduce

microscopic So small that it can be seen only by using a microscope

migrate To travel to another area for food or to reproduce

minerals Natural substances that help plants and animals grow

mutualistic relationship A relationship between two or more species that benefits or helps both species

nutrients Substances that allow organisms to thrive and grow

oceanographers Scientists who study oceans

oil spills The accidental dumping of large amounts of oil into oceans organisms Living things

photosynthesis The process in which plants use sunlight to change carbon dioxide and water into food and oxygen

pollutants Harmful substances

populations The total numbers of certain species in an area

precipitation Water that falls from the clouds as rain, snow, sleet, or hail

predators Animals that hunt other animals for food

pressure The force that pushes on or against an object

prey An animal that is hunted by another animal for food

reproduce To produce offspring

sea ice Frozen water that floats on the surface of polar oceans in huge sheets

species A group of animals or plants that are similar and can produce young

tides The rise and fall of ocean water

tropical Describing a hot and humid climate

tropics A hot, humid region of Earth found near the equator between the Tropic of Cancer and the Tropic of Capricorn

water column An area of water from the surface to the bottom

Learning More

Find out more about Earth's precious ocean ecosystems.

Books

Benoit, Peter. *Oceans* (A True Book). New York, NY: Scholastic, 2011.

Gazlay, Suzy. *Re-Greening the Environment: Careers in Clean-up, Remediation, and Renewal*. St. New York, NY: Crabtree Publishing Company, 2011.

Owen, Ruth. *Marine Biologists* (Out of the Lab: Extreme Jobs in Science). New York, NY: Powerkids Press, 2013.

Websites

This National Geographic website explores a variety of marine ecosystems:
http://education.nationalgeographic.com/education/media/marine-ecosystem-illustrations-grades-3-5/?ar_a=1

This fun site from NASA invites you to play games and make things while you find out about oceans and the world's climate:
http://climatekids.nasa.gov/menu/ocean

Follow this link to discover marine and freshwater ecosystems and the world's biomes:
www.mbgnet.net/salt

Dive into this website to learn more about marine ecosystems:
http://kids.nceas.ucsb.edu/biomes/marine.html

Index